Dewey
&
The Lady's Slipper

Gail Timberlake
With Betsy Healey

Dot Samuel, Illustrator

Fluvanna County Public Library
214 Commons Blvd.
Palmyra, VA 22963

AuthorHouse™ LLC
1663 Liberty Drive
Bloomington, IN 47403
www.authorhouse.com
Phone: 1-800-839-8640

© 2014 Gail Timberlake. All rights reserved.

No part of this book may be reproduced, stored in a retrieval system, or
transmitted by any means without the written permission of the author.

Published by AuthorHouse 02/04/2014

ISBN: 978-1-4918-5735-9 (sc)
978-1-4918-5736-6 (e)

Library of Congress Control Number: 2014901535

Any people depicted in stock imagery provided by Thinkstock are models,
and such images are being used for illustrative purposes only.
Certain stock imagery © Thinkstock.

This book is printed on acid-free paper.

Because of the dynamic nature of the Internet, any web addresses or links contained in this book may have changed
since publication and may no longer be valid. The views expressed in this work are solely those of the author and do
not necessarily reflect the views of the publisher, and the publisher hereby disclaims any responsibility for them.

To my God who has richly blessed me with a multitude of friends. This book is dedicated to the loving memory of my batteau friends who now live in my heart. May their spirits inspire each of us as long as Virginia's river's flow.

Gail Timberlake
Author

In Memory of:

Virginia D King	Dave Welchon
Gail Felts	Freddie Crance
Karen Abse	VG Bailey
Stedman Grey	Dave Griener
Dewey Wood	Nancy Trout
Dana Williams	John McFadden
"Gini" Norconk Zirckle	Jimmy Timberlake, my sweetheart
Cliff Brown	John Lewis

Words of wisdom were offered concerning names of batteau friends that may not have been submitted for this book. My best effort was put into gathering names for months. Please accept apologies if you know of someone that was not included. Write their name in the margin in bold print to honor their memory and please overlook my shortcomings. My intent was to include any and all names provided to me. Names appear in the order I received them.

To God's amazing grace and to my husband, David, the "strong and gentle" man in my life who is so supportive of me and shares my love of the river.

Dot Samuel
illustrator

Special thanks to my youngest grandsons, Mason and Clayton Timberlake for their artwork found in the back of the book. Their energy and enthusiasm has prompted me to have hope, keep moving forward and write a few more books.

Foreword

Dewey Wood was a gentle giant born in Schuyler, Virginia on July 28, 1955. One could not think of the James River Batteau Festival without thinking of him. The festival and Dewey were synonymous with each other. His love for the outdoors was one of his greatest passions. The batteaux were part of his life for 20 years. His legacy is commemorated with a plaque placed on the face of a rock near the confluence of the Tye and James River in Buckingham County, Virginia. Another tribute is the "Dewey Pole" which is awarded to a boat program that exemplifies service to others and overall goodwill.

He was a happy-go-lucky man with a big heart as well as a laugh and smile that were contagious. Children loved him—adults who knew him counted him as a blessing.

Dewey embraced life to the fullest having fun in everything he did. One could not find a finer carpenter, butcher, cow chaser, cook, window cleaner, batteau man, woodcutter or stone/brick mason. He could fix anything that was broken. He was also an athlete—baseball, football, basketball, track, horseshoes, pool, horseback riding and even croquet.

He was a Jaycee, a helper and a volunteer. He was loved and he loved—a true friend.

Dewey S. Wood   7/28/1955 - 5/23/2007

The crew of the *Lady's Slipper* rounded the point of the landing on their left up into the Rockfish River at Howardsville. I always enjoyed the campsite where the Rockfish flows into the James River. I loved the little store, the people, and particularly the rocky beach. We played on this beach each year on the fourth day of the James River Batteau Festival.

Tuesday, Roger, co-owner of the Howardsville canoe & livery had arranged a three hour tubing excursion.

Most of my family spent the afternoon lazily relaxing on old inner-tubes from "Sunnyside" right up onto the rocky beach in Howardsville. Rather than tubing, my daughter, Joy and I chose to be crew members on our batteau, the *Lady's Slipper*.

From the "*Slipper*" I shouted at Mason and Clayton (my two youngest grandsons) cautioning them "Stay clear of the boats!"

We poled into an opening among dozens of canoes, kayaks, and batteaux.

"Hi, Nana!" Mason yelled with excitement.

Both boys came running toward us carrying rocks as well as a bucket of sand they wanted to show me.

"Nana, can we wear our batteau clothes and coon skin hats, now?" Clayton asked me. "And I want to wear my moccasins, too!" Mason quickly added.

Each of them gave me a big hug. Aunt Joy got a kiss on the cheek as we headed to the campsite to dry off and help the kids change into their period clothing. Mason came out of the camper carrying a magazine in his hand.

I recognized the publication as an old copy of the **Tiller**. I usually kept this one with my picture albums and journal that I had written in since the first festival in June of 1986. The cover had a photograph of Dewey Wood posing on the front sweep of his batteau, the *Maple Run.* This **Tiller** held sentimental value—to me it was priceless.

Clayton began to ask questions such as "Who is this, what's the name of his batteau, and can we meet him?"

"That is my dear friend, Dewey Wood", I replied as my mind was flooded with fond memories. "Dewey died tragically in 2007. He was a true friend to the *Lady's Slipper.*"

Clayton continued to quiz me. He seemed quite curious about this big, strong man. "How can he be a friend if he has gone to Heaven? What did he do to help your batteau?"

I responded, as I recalled the countless ways Dewey helped others "Well, Dewey was a friend to all the crew members on all the batteaux, not just the *'Slipper'.*"

"Tell you what, boys," I said. "Let's go talk with Captain Betsy at the Schlepper. She was on the *'Slipper'* one year when the river was so high, it was almost too dangerous to continue the festival on the James. Dewey was the key person to maneuver three batteaux through a critical situation!"

Mason ran ahead of me, greeted Captain Betsy and wrapped one arm around her legs. Still excited, he thrust the **Tiller** up into her view asking her to tell him all about Dewey Wood. "Nana says Dewey knew how to help everybody!"

"Indeed, he did!" she responded. "Tell us about the high water, Capt Betsy!" Clayton squealed, hardly able to contain himself.

Captain Betsy began with "Dewey could put a plan together, organize and carry it out with little or no effort! The second day of the 2003 festival could have been a complete disaster. Thanks to Dewey, it wasn't a disaster, but a delight for the crew members of the *Maple Run*, the *Cartersville of Columbia*, and the *Lady's Slipper*.

Our crew had chosen to go river left around Pettyjohn Island. We were moving way too fast to pole. We could see other batteaux a great distance ahead sensing something was awry. As we approached the scene, we observed crew members waving their arms frantically.

Our imaginations ran wild. There appeared to be a huge tree across the James.

Upon closer examination of the situation we realized we needed to slow the '*Slipper*' down! It wasn't a tree after all! We were going to crash into a bridge and two other batteaux if we did not act quickly! Barbara, on the front sweep, cut really hard to the right breaking the walk board off. We managed to stop our boat about 50 yards from the bridge before anyone was hurt.

Dewey, his crew and some of the crew of the other boat were standing on the bridge. Several people were up on the river bank, too. Each of us were relieved that calamity had been avoided!

On this particular day, Dewey was full of himself and all life had to offer. He was all smiles, laughter and jokes. He orchestrated a plan giving each of us a part to play. The harmony was beautiful.

It was obvious that the batteaux were not going to pass under the low bridge. The canopy of the *'Slipper'* was especially tall. The first step was to unload and portage supplies along with all the equipment. It was helpful at this point to lighten our load. To accomplish this our crew fed the entire group leaving us with less 'stuff' when the time came to re-load. Our reputation for excellent cuisine always resulted in a well fed bunch of 'river rats.' Gratitude was expressed as we prepared for another task.

Next, he directed everyone to sink their boats! The ladies retrieved buckets and containers to begin the process of filling our boat with water.

Dewey had a better idea, one that would be much more efficient and less time consuming. He quietly suggested to the ladies that we simply stand on the "gunnels". Immediately, people lined up on one side of the '*Slipper*' and down she went.

  I distinctly remember telling all involved that I was going to vote for Dewey Wood as the next President of the United States of America! This man made hard tasks and difficult situations appear to be so simple to handle. A job that would seem daunting to others, Dewey turned into fun.

The third step was to use a rope to guide the batteaux under the bridge in the swift current. The entire episode took about 1 ½ hours to complete. Imagine that—only 90 minutes to unload, sink, guide under the bridge, bail out and reload three batteaux and all their crew!

Dewey's leadership style was 'Everybody helps Everybody.' He led us through it with no blood, sweat or tears—only laughter accompanied with easy camaraderie."

Captain Betsy finished her story saying, "Even today, over a decade later, I find myself in awe of our friend, Dewey. I marvel at how an incredibly strong man--with all his history, pride in his masculinity and his race--could embody such a gentle and caring spirit. He was so comfortable and confident in those pink, rubber river shoes!"

The boys listened attentively throughout the time Captain Betsy reminisced. I found myself a little choked up as I recalled the friendship of Dewey Wood and his valuable contributions to the JRBF family.

Captain smiled at the boys, ending the storytelling with a question for them "What are some ways you can be a friend to a batteau crew?"

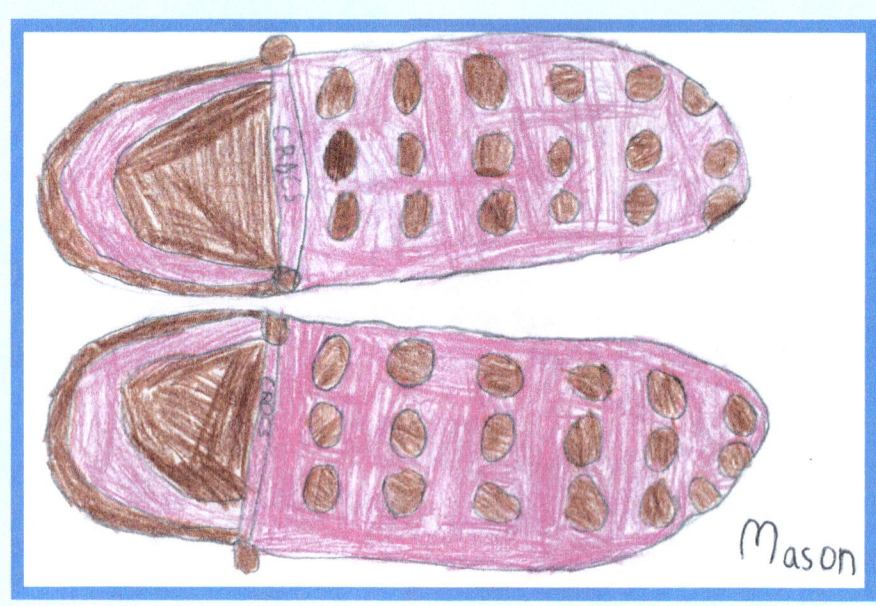

Matthew 25:23

Mark 12:31

The Ballad of Dewey Wood

Where the Rockfish runs down to the mighty River James
There was a man, Dewey Wood was his name
With the rivers in his blood he was a great bear of a man
To those in trouble on the streams he would always lend a hand.

Dewey was a carpenter 'tween the Rockfish and the Tye
All the ladies loved his smile, as broad as the river is wide
But the thing that he loved best of all were the rivers and the streams
And floating down their currents ran through Dewey's fondest dreams.

When the spring turns into summer on the river James' shore
The long batteau put in and go to recall times from before
The Sam Cabell and the Rose of Nelson carried Dewey Wood
He poled and swept and laughed and played on the mighty river's flood.

From Lynchburg down to Maidens Dewey taught us what he knew
Just follow the trash & watch the stream & your batteau will run through
He saved the Lady's Slipper as she sank into the mud
A kindly man who would lend a hand with a smile was Dewey Wood.

Now all we have are the memories of a man who was so good
An angry man with a gun in hand has taken Dewey Wood
But his batteau pole is carried on the River James with pride
And a plaque is there with Dewey's name on a stone on the riverside.

Put your boat in at Wingina and float past the river's shore
In the early light you may see a sight that will make your spirit soar
Right over Dewey's name you just might see a great black bear
And we know that Dewey's spirit watches over us right there.

When the spring turns into summer on the mighty River James
The batteau folk will pole their boats and remember Dewey's name
They'll lift a glass to the great black bear of a man they used to know
Whose spirit will live on as long as Virginia's river's flow.

Written by Rhonda Baker, Lady's Slipper crew member
(Permission granted to include in this publication -2013)

Glossary

Awry	–	wrong
Batteau(x)	–	French word for long boat used to carry goods on the river during the late 1700s
Camaraderie	–	warm, friendly feeling
Caution	–	a warning
Critical	–	dangerous or risky
Cuisine	–	the food prepared
Daunting	–	discouraging or disheartening
Frantically	–	wild with worry
Gunnels	–	the upper edge of the side of a boat or ship
JRBF	–	see back cover for definition
Lady's Slipper	–	an orchid with flowers somewhat like slippers
Maneuver	–	planned and controlled movement
Portage	–	carrying of goods overland
Publication	–	usually a book, magazine, newspaper, etc.
Reminisce	–	to think, talk, or write about past experiences
Schlepper	–	to drag, the trailer used to carry supplies
Sentimental	–	having or showing tender feelings
Tiller	–	Virginia Canals & Navigations Society magazine

CPSIA information can be obtained at www.ICGtesting.com
Printed in the USA
BVOW10s0307260214

346014BV00001B/1/P